Butch Cassidy & The Sundance Kid: The Lives and Legacies of the Wild West's Famous Outlaw Duo

By Charles River Editors

About Charles River Editors

Charles River Editors was founded by Harvard and MIT alumni to provide superior editing and original writing services, with the expertise to create digital content for publishers across a vast range of subject matter. In addition to providing original digital content for third party publishers, Charles River Editors republishes civilization's greatest literary works, bringing them to a new generation via ebooks.

Sign up here to receive updates about free books as we publish them, and visit Our Kindle Author Page to browse today's free promotions and our most recently published Kindle titles.

Introduction

Butch Cassidy (1866-1908) and Sundance Kid (1867-1908)

The Wild West has made legends out of many men through the embellishment of their stories, such as crediting Billy the Kid and Wild Bill Hickok for killing far more people than they actually did. But it has also made icons out of outlaws like Butch Cassidy and the Sundance Kid based on the mystery and uncertainty surrounding their crimes and deaths, allowing speculation and legend to fill in the gaps.

Though Butch Cassidy and the Sundance Kid are the two most famous members of the Wild Bunch and will probably always be associated with each other, there's no indication that they had any particularly close friendship or relationship aside from being members of the same gang. In fact, they might not have been linked together at all but for the fact that they both chose to flee the country for Argentina to escape justice. It was in South America that the famous outlaws are believed to have met their ultimate fate in a shootout with Bolivian soldiers, but the mystery and controversy surrounding that shootout (and whether the two bandits were actually them) have helped ensure their place in Western lore. As with so many other legends of the West, people continue to speculate that Butch Cassidy and the Sundance Kid survived and lived out the rest of their lives.

In fact, it was in South America that Butch Cassidy and the Sundance Kid are believed to have met their ultimate fate in a shootout with Bolivian soldiers. The mystery and controversy surrounding that shootout (and whether the two bandits were actually them) have helped ensure their place in Western lore, and as with so many other legends of the West, people continue to speculate that Butch Cassidy and the Sundance Kid survived and lived out the rest of their lives.

Butch Cassidy & The Sundance Kid chronicles the outlaws' lives, while also analyzing their legacies and mythology that have enveloped their stories, in an attempt to separate fact from fiction and determine what the notorious robbers were really like. Along with pictures of important people and places, you will learn about Butch and Sundance like never before.

Butch Cassidy & The Sundance Kid: The Lives and Legacies of the Wild West's Famous Outlaw Duo

About Charles River Editors

Introduction

Chapter 1: Bob Parker

Chapter 2: Harry Longabaugh

Chapter 3: The Sundance Kid

Chapter 4: The Telluride Bank Robbery

Chapter 5: Wyoming State Penitentiary

Chapter 6: Butch, Sundance, and the Wild Bunch

Great Northern Express Train Robbery

Montpelier, Idaho

Castle Gate, Utah

Belle Fourche

Elko, Nevada

Wilcox, Wyoming

Cassidy's Attempt at Amnesty

Chapter 7: Heading to South America

Chapter 8: The End of the Road?

Chapter 9: The Legacy of Butch and Sundance

Bibliography

Chapter 1: Bob Parker

Robert LeRoy Parker was born in Beaver, Utah on April 13, 1866, just shy of 20 years after Brigham Young led a band of Mormons to Salt Lake City in pursuit of a location to freely practice their religion, far from persecution and scrutiny over their practice of polygamy. Parker was named after his grandfather, an Englishman who led a group of determined Mormon refugees, later known as the Handcart Pioneers, thousands of miles on foot over the Plains, mountainous terrain, and the desert into Utah.

In the late 1850s, that Robert Parker, his wife Ann, and his oldest son, 12 year old Maximilian, walked along the Mormon Trail, pulling all of their belongings in wooden handcarts. Parker was a strong man and a natural leader, making him an obvious choice to take a front position as his group began its journey from Iowa to Utah. However, there was some concern about the weather they would encounter. Leaving Iowa in late August or early September meant the group might very well encounter snow before they reached Salt Lake City, but Parker and the rest of the group put their faith in Brigham Young. He assured them that the Lord would watch over them and keep the snow at bay until they arrived safely.

By mid-October, the pioneers reached the Continental Divide, and, predictably, snow blasted the mountains. Parker led the way and helped break through snowdrifts to clear passage for his family and others, but with a warmer valley in sight, Parker was found dead one morning, still wrapped in his blankets. Young Maximilian dug as deep of a grave as he could in the freezing ground and laid his father to rest before he trudged on toward Utah with the rest of the cold and starving pioneers. When they finally made it to their destination, Max had his first taste of watermelon.

Max and his mother settled at American Fork, about 30 miles south of Salt Lake City. In 1865, they moved to Beaver, and he married Ann Campbell, raising their 13 children in Circleville. Robert, called Bob by most people, was the oldest. When Bob was still a young boy, Max bought a ranch 12 miles south of Circleville, not far from what is now Bryce Canyon National Park. The ranch was known to attract its share of cowboys and cattle rustlers, including an outlaw named Mike Cassidy.

Cassidy, who worked as a cowhand on the ranch, made quite an impression on Bob and taught him some of the most important skills a man of the West could learn, including how to shoot a gun, how to ride a horse, and how to rope, brand, and rustle cattle. For those reasons, contemporaries believed Bob could have had a career as a rancher if he wanted one, and some speculate that he later fronted as a rancher to hide his clandestine, illegal activities. Parker was good with horses and by the time he was 16, he was known as the best shot in Circleville.

Bob grew into a strong, stocky young man, and he was known to be quick-witted and charming. Like Cassidy, he was friendly and jovial much of the time, and just about anyone who encountered him took a liking to him. Not surprisingly, when Butch Cassidy and the Sundance Kid became popular heroes in movies and on television, the two were also turned into a comedic team, needling each other with running dialogue. In one memorable scene from the famous 1969 movie *Butch Cassidy and the Sundance Kid*, Butch says to Sundance, "Is that what you call giving cover?" In response, Sundance retorts, "Is that what you call running?"

Bob's personality is one of the few aspects about his life on which people agree. Indeed, it is not clear when or why Bob developed his disdain for authority and the law. It may have been following an incident between his father and the local Mormon church. The church bishop served as the authority in the community and ruled against Max in a property dispute, leaving the family to have to take odd jobs to try to make ends meet. It may have also been when Bob stole a saddle and was jailed by the sheriff of Garfield County, who some say did not treat the young man well and inadvertently set him on his path toward becoming an outlaw. It can also be safely said that daily interactions with men like Mike Cassidy and outlaws on the ranch had some influence too. Ranching was hard work and it did not take long for Bob to see that there were easier ways to make a living. Mike Cassidy was a hero to Bob, and it is not a stretch to suggest that he heavily influenced him, especially since Parker ended up taking Cassidy's last name as an alias.

At the same time, Bob was never actually a violent man, at least not in the manner that many other Western icons were known to be. He did not hold personal grudges against the lawmen that chased him most of his life, there is no documented evidence that he actually ever killed a man, and he rarely used his gun unless someone shot at him first. In an era where men like Wild Bill Hickok and Doc Holliday allowed exaggerated reports of their kill count so that their reputation preceded them and made them safe, Butch Cassidy did the exact opposite. In fact, Cassidy and the Wild Bunch gang actually tried to downplay their violence and bragged (falsely) that they made every effort to avoid shooting people.

One popular story has Cassidy showing his humanity early on in his career as a criminal when he was arrested for stealing horses near Circleville. According to the legend, Bob did not resist and easily went along with the two men who arrested him. It was a long ride to the county jail and they stopped for lunch when they came across some shade trees near a stream. Bob, who had presented no problems to the deputies but was still handcuffed, watched as one of the men turned toward the stream to dip a bucket in for water. Bob suddenly pushed the officer into the stream. Before the officers realized what was happening, Bob had both of their guns, the handcuff keys, and took off with not only the horses he had already stolen, but their horses, too. He didn't get too far down the trail, though, when he realized that he had all of the canteens. Bob turned around and gave the lawmen the canteens so that they could fill them with water for their walk back to town, telling them that he knew what it was like to be in the desert without water.

Another way that Bob was different from other icons of the West (except perhaps for young Billy the Kid) is that he was never much of a drinker. If he did indulge, he was known to have a taste of "the good stuff" and liked a drink of Mount Vernon whiskey or Old Crow. Those who met him said he was a man of his word. He did like his freedom, though, and he did not like rules. For that reason, Bob knew early that he could not live a life on the straight and narrow path, and he admitted as much to those who urged him to reconsider his ways. His reasons for becoming an outlaw seemed to be tied to his desire to be free from constraints. Bob wanted to make his own rules.

Chapter 2: Harry Longabaugh

Josiah Longabaugh was a native of Pennsylvania, as was his father, Jonas. They were descendants of Conrad Langenbach, whose ship from Germany arrived in Philadelphia on Christmas Eve in 1772, but like many immigrants of the colonial era, Langenbach was an indentured servant. By the time he had worked long enough to pay for his passage to America, he was able to enlist in the Continental Army and serve in the Revolutionary War with the Northampton County Militia, after which he settled northeast of Philadelphia in rural Pennsylvania. By then, Conrad's last name had morphed into Longabaugh, and he had taken a wife named Catharina, with whom he had seven children.

Conrad's great-grandson Josiah was not as ambitious as he was. Josiah was never able to keep a job for long and never owned any land, and though he was drafted into the Civil War to serve for the Union Army, he was discharged due to a chronic case of hemorrhoids. His wife Christiana, however, was a religious woman who ran an orderly household, and together they had five children: Elwood, Samanna, Emma, Harvey, Harry. The one destined to be one of the West's most notorious outlaws became the youngest child sometime in the spring of 1867.

As Josiah moved from job to job, the family moved from rental house to rental house, but they never strayed far from Mont Clare or Phoenixville, Pennsylvania. When Harry was born, the Longabaugh family lived in a duplex near the Schuylkill Canal, an area that drew immigrants who could find jobs at the Phoenix Iron Company, the local mill in Phoenixville. The town was prosperous, largely due to the board of directors of the mill, who devoted time and money to improving the town. The mill also made a cannon named for its inventor, John Griffen, which was known as one of the finest of its kind.

Harry's grandfather, Harry Place, was a deacon at the First Baptist Church in Phoenixville, which Harry attended from time to time. But it doesn't seem like the young boy took to religion quite like his mother. The Longabaughs had regular family gatherings on holidays, birthdays, and picnics, and those that recalled young Sundance said he was of "unsettled spirit" and seemed as if he would rather be somewhere other than with his family. By the age of 13, he would be.

Whether it was due to financial reasons or the restless spirit his family noticed, Harry moved out on his own and in 1880 was a boarder at Wilmer Ralston's farm in West Vincent. Given his age, it's most likely that Harry worked for Ralston in exchange for room and board.

At 14 years of age, Harry and his uncle took a canal boat to Philadelphia, and then moved on to Boston and New York to find jobs. Harry apparently did not find suitable employment because that same August, his sister Samanna noted in her journal that he left to go to "the West." Heading for the frontier, Harry took a train from Phoenixville to Cortez, Colorado to help a distant cousin named George Longenbaugh. New land had opened up to homesteaders in Colorado, and George had packed a covered wagon with all of his belongings and moved his wife and son to Cortez to start a new life there. After he invited his teenager cousin to join them, Harry stayed there for a few years until 1886, helping out with planting crops, breeding horses, and general maintenance on the property. The horse ranching skills that Harry learned came in handy later and allowed him to find jobs on horse ranches many times when he found himself in need of work.

Not far away from Cortez was a man that would become forever linked with Harry. About 75 miles north of Cortez is Telluride, once a booming mining town but also a popular location for horse racing. Robert Leroy Parker, who would later become known as Butch Cassidy, lived in Telluride, where he was also the co-owner of a racehorse. While it can't be known for certain, the future Sundance Kid may have met the future Butch Cassidy on the horse racing circuit around 1885.

At 19, Harry was ready to strike out on his own and migrated north of Colorado and into Wyoming. It was spring, and Harry was by now such an experienced horse trainer that he had little difficulty finding work as a horse wrangler. For $35 a month, Harry worked for the Suffolk Cattle Company, doing the physically demanding work of breaking horses at the AV Ranch located along the Cheyenne River. Harry was good at his work, but he also quickly earned a reputation for having a quick temper. In his first week on the ranch, he mixed it up with three other ranch hands and was ready to fight the cook for mocking his last name by calling him "Longboy." Not surprisingly, with outbursts like that Harry didn't last at the ranch for long.

Exactly how long Harry worked for Suffolk and Company is not certain, but his departure may have been hastened by his arrest for a robbery in nearby Lusk, Wyoming, where a distant cousin happened to live. An elderly man was robbed of $80, and Harry was reportedly taken into custody by the local sheriff, but the robber escaped from the county jail that same night.

Chapter 3: The Sundance Kid

In February 1887, Harry was working at the N Bar N in Culbertson, Montana. At the time, the Three V Ranch was located in the northeast corner of Wyoming where it borders South Dakota and Montana, and a road between the Black Hills of South Dakota and the N Bar N went directly through the Three V Ranch. Harry was known to travel along that road.

The winter quarters and horse camp for the Three V Ranch was on Crow Creek, a wide-open range north of the town of Sundance, Wyoming. John Clay, the manager of the ranch, was the president of the Wyoming Stock Growers Association and a member of a playground for Cheyenne's most wealthy citizens, the Cheyenne Club. Built in 1880, the club counted many British investors as its members. The three-story building featured wine vaults, tennis courts, dining and smoking rooms, and a group of private rooms that no doubt saw their share of underground games of chance.

On February 27, as Harry passed through the Three V Ranch, he helped himself to a saddle, a revolver, and a horse sporting the brand "J". While Harry moved on to Miles City, employees of the Three V Ranch began a two week search for the thief with no luck. James Widner, who worked for the ranch, met with Sheriff James Ryan in the closest county seat to file theft charges. Ryan served as sheriff of Crook County in Sundance, Wyoming, and when word got to Ryan that Harry had been arrested outside of Miles City in possession of the stolen goods, he went to Miles City to pick him up. On April 8, 1887, arrest papers were filed and Harry was detained in the local jail.

For reasons that are unclear, the sheriff took a rather lengthy route back to Sundance, which included a pass through St. Paul, Minnesota. All of the extra stops on a trip that took 2,000 miles (when Sundance was only 300 miles from Miles City) gave Harry a chance to escape in Duluth, Minnesota. When Ryan was in the train's restroom, Harry picked the lock of his shackles and leapt off the moving train. Some say that he had help in his escape, possibly from Butch Cassidy, but however he did it, Harry would later prove that his escape from the train was no fluke.

Upon realizing that his prisoner was gone, Ryan ordered the conductor to stop the train and thoroughly searched all of the cars until he was convinced that Harry had indeed vanished. When he got back to Wyoming, Ryan issued a reward of $250 for Harry's capture, and it did not take long to find the fugitive. Perhaps still young and naïve, Harry returned to Miles City, and on June 6 he was arrested by Sheriff Eph K. Davis and Inspector W. Smith in Montana at the N Bar Ranch. After Davis and Smith relieved Harry of his two six-shooters, he was chained to the wall of a shack, where they planned to wait for the next stagecoach to pass by the next day.

Davis and Smith were well aware that Harry was something of an escape artist. As they settled in the shack for the night, Davis went to one corner and Smith to the other, with Harry between them. Smith fell asleep but Davis just pretended to doze off while he waited to see what Harry might do. Right on cue, Harry picked the locks of his shackles again. As he rose up to his feet and moved to the window, he heard Davis calmly say, "Kid, you're loose, ain't you."[1] With that, Harry went back to his spot along the wall. When Sheriff Ryan eventually took Harry back into

---

[1] Donna Ernst, *The Sundance Kid: The Life of Harry Alonzo Longabaugh,* Page 36.

custody, he prepared for the stagecoach ride back to Sundance by securing Harry in steel handcuffs that were reinforced with steel rivets.

Harry and Ryan arrived in Sundance on June 22, 1887. Harry either lied about his age and said he was 26 or the clerk made an error because he was still only 20. Court records listed his occupation as cowboy. He was said to have no parents (although his father was still alive), no religion, no children, and the space for education was marked "common." Having already escaped once and tried a second time, the brash youngster warned Ryan that he was going to try and escape yet again, and he kept his word. With the help of a fellow inmate, he managed to remove a bolt from his jail cell door, but it was discovered before he had a chance to get away. In exchange for a guilty plea, two of the three charges against him were dropped and he was sentenced to 18 months hard labor. Because of his age, he served his jail term at the Crook County Jail, the new building that had recently gone up behind the county courthouse.

On February 4, 1889, the day before he was due to be released, Governor Thomas Moonlight issued Harry a full pardon, although it is not known that Harry was aware of this. It is also not clear why he did not take the chance that was offered him to live a clean life. He was obviously a skilled cowboy and horseman, but there was something that drew him to the outlaw's life instead. The time Harry spent in jail would lead to his famous nickname, but it would not reform him.

Harry's release from jail was not the end of his exploits in Sundance. He stayed in the northeast Wyoming region for a while until he found himself in trouble again. On May 24, 1889, Harry was arrested for the murders of Sheriff E.B. Armstrong and Deputy Sheriff James Swisher. The lawmen had come across Harry, an outlaw named Buck Hanby, and two other men about 35 miles from Sundance. Hanby was wanted for a murder in Greeley County, Kansas, and when the men were told to put their hands in the air, Hanby shot Armstrong and Swisher. However, Hanby swore out a complaint against Harry, who by then was known as Kid Longabaugh to many. Harry was arrested on May 24, but the trail ends there, and it's unclear when he was released, why he was released, or even whether he escaped. In any case, Harry would never forget his time in Sundance, the small town that gave him his famous nickname. Kid Longabaugh became the Sundance Kid.

Chapter 4: The Telluride Bank Robbery

Facts about Bob Parker's early life are sketchy, but most historians agree that he worked as a rancher around the West until about 1884, and he seems to have briefly worked as a butcher in Rock Springs, Wyoming, giving him the nickname Butch. Whether he took Cassidy as his last name to protect the Parker family name or out of hero worship for Mike Cassidy is not clear, but either way he was known at this time in his life as George "Butch" Cassidy. Over the course of his life, he would have numerous aliases.

For a man destined to become one of the West's most famous outlaws, the first charge brought against Parker was incredibly trivial. In or around 1880, the teenager went to buy clothes and some food from one of the shops in town, but when he arrived he found it was closed. Refusing to leave without what he came for, he took a pair of jeans and pie, and in their place he left an IOU note letting the owner know he would pay for the goods next time he came to the shop. In response, the shopkeeper filed a charge against the kid. A jury later acquitted him.

Telluride is on the western slopes of the San Juan Mountains in southwestern Colorado, and when Cassidy arrived in 1889, it was a wild mining town filled with prospectors lured by the dream of finding gold in the nearby hills. As was the case with all mining towns, whiskey flowed easily in Telluride, and men looked to the gambling halls, saloons, and brothels to blow off steam. Furthermore, the San Miguel Valley Bank was a tempting lure to potential bank robbers. The small wooden building did not look like much from the outside, but in an attempt to impress investors, the interior was lavishly decorated. Years later, Matt Warner said, "I didn't know before that there was any place in the world with such rich trimmings and furnishings as the inside of that bank."[2] Naturally, that same interior impressed those looking to withdraw money from the bank too, especially those who didn't have an account there.

Warner met Cassidy somewhere along the way before the scheme to rob the San Miguel bank was devised. The two men partnered on the ownership of a race horse named Betty and stole livestock, among other things. In the days leading up to the robbery, Warner, Cassidy, and Tom McCarty were seen freely spending money around town, giving no signs of being men in need of cash. Speculation is that the money they were spending came courtesy of a robbery in Denver, but they also spent money intentionally as part of their plan. According to Warner, they wanted to seem like they were in town to have a good time, not to case the local bank.

The morning of June 24, 1889, four men checked their horses out of the local livery and patronized the saloons near the San Miguel Valley Bank. At noon, bank employee Charlie Painter left the bank, leaving only one teller remaining on duty. Two of the four robbers waited outside of the bank with the horses and the other two robbers went inside. One of the bandits told the teller that he wanted to cash a check and when the teller took a closer look, the bandit shoved his face into the desk and told him to keep quiet. The other three robbers entered the bank and scooped up all of the money they could find. For unknown reasons, they did not wear masks or try to shield their identity. Exact accounts of the robbery and Cassidy's role vary, but within minutes, the men took off with over $20,000. In addition to McCarty, Warner, and Cassidy, the fourth man has been speculated to be any number of outlaws, including Harry Longabaugh (the Sundance Kid) and Dan Parker, Butch Cassidy's brother. It may also have been one of McCarty's brothers.

---

[2] Patterson, Richard. *Butch Cassidy: A Biography.* Page 21.

On their way out of town, the robbers crossed paths with two other men from town. The men recognized Warner and Cassidy, a mistake that Warner claims set them on their path as outlaws for good because it made sure that they were always on the run. Warner also said that McCarty commented after they continued down the trail that he should have shot the two men.

Though there has been speculation that Sundance participated in the bank robbery at Telluride, it's not likely. From Wyoming, he went to Montana near Lavina and started working for the John T. Murphy Cattle Company, and in the spring of 1890 he traveled just south of the Canadian border to northeastern Montana, working on a ranch as a horse breaker. In fact, it was not until 1892 that reports of the Sundance Kid being in trouble with the law reappear. But with that said, he spent much of his time in the Rocky Mountain West, and it is assumed that he came to know at least some of the men that formed the Wild Bunch during these years.

Chapter 5: Wyoming State Penitentiary

After the Telluride robbery, it is believed that Cassidy and his fellow outlaws hid out at Robbers Roost in southeastern Utah. The remote area made it an ideal hiding place for outlaws because it was difficult to get to and easy to defend if a lawman was so bold as to approach. As it would turn out, no members of law enforcement even knew of its existence until after Cassidy's death. Given that Cassidy and his gang built cabins there and stored cattle, horses, and assorted weaponry, it is safe to assume that Robbers Roost was used frequently, and that the outlaws may have even used the area during winters. The area was made famous again a century later when hiker Aron Ralston amputated his own arm to free himself from an 800-pound boulder. His story was the subject of the 2011 movie, *127 Hours*.

In 1890, Cassidy bought a ranch near Dubois, Wyoming, and in 1894, he began a sporadic relationship with a teenage girl named Ann Bassett, the daughter of a local and prominent cattle rancher named Herb Bassett. Ann's sister, Josie, was also known to have a relationship with another of Cassidy's associates and future member of the Wild Bunch, Elzy Lay. Ann and Josie were considered to be intelligent women who also knew the ranching business. Their father did business with Cassidy, and it is speculated that part of the motivation for the sisters to have romantic relationships with Cassidy and Lay, as well as other Cassidy associates, was to keep other outlaws from harassing them. Women were rarely allowed to visit the hideout at Robbers Roost, but Ann and Josie were two of the ones that spent time there.

Ann Bassett

Elzy Lay

The other famous hideout for Cassidy and his gang, which came to be known as the Wild Bunch, was Hole-in-the-Wall north of Casper, Wyoming. It was ideal for ranchers thanks to the open grazing land, but the remote location and one-way entry also made it a good hideout. In addition, Cassidy's gang spent time at Brown's Hole, a canyon located near the Green River, where the borders of Utah, Wyoming, and Colorado meet.

The site of Hole-in-the-Wall

Cassidy, for the only time in his life, found himself behind bars in 1894. Whether he was living the life of a law-abiding citizen or he simply had not been caught, he had managed to stay out of trouble with the law for nearly four years, but he was eventually arrested for stealing horses. He may have been arrested and released for insufficient evidence prior to this, but this time he was taken to Lander, Wyoming for a trial and convicted. Cassidy was sentenced to two years in the Wyoming State Penitentiary in Laramie. Legend has it that Cassidy asked the local sheriff if he could leave for the night, promising to return the next morning to serve his prison sentence. Even more incredibly, the sheriff not only agreed but even let Cassidy use his horse. Legend had it that Cassidy used the opportunity to say farewell to Ann Bassett before serving his time. If the story is true, Cassidy must have kept his word because he was certainly a prisoner in the Wyoming State Penitentiary.

Cassidy, whose occupation was listed as "cowboy" in his prison file, was on his best behavior in prison. He petitioned Wyoming Governor William Richards for an early release, and Richards reportedly agreed to let him go if Cassidy would stay out of trouble in Wyoming. Cassidy was released from prison on January 19, 1896 and from there, he promptly went to either Hole-in-the-Wall or Brown's Hole.

Chapter 6: Butch, Sundance, and the Wild Bunch

Great Northern Express Train Robbery

Although Butch and Sundance had taken part in various crimes during the first half the 1890s, the gang that they came to be associated with did not really begin its crime spree until 1896. It was in January of that year that Butch Cassidy was released from the Wyoming Territorial Prison, the only prison term he would ever serve, and after his release the Wild Bunch began to truly develop. Cassidy joined forces with Sundance, George "Flat Nose" Curry, and any number of at least 30 different men who came and went from Cassidy's gang.

The Wild Bunch is as much myth as it is fact, and they certainly never called themselves the Wild Bunch. In fact, it was not until the Pinkerton Detective Agency called them the Wild Bunch that anyone had ever heard the name. As many as 30 different men have been linked to the gang at various times, but very few of them committed more than one or two holdups with each other. It's also unclear how many crimes they were actually responsible for and just how many Butch Cassidy and Sundance Kid actively participated in. It's altogether possible that Sundance had never even met Cassidy before he was released from jail in 1896, and only three heists can be linked back to them, but the gang's reputation would be firmly established, and Cassidy and Sundance would soon become two of the most wanted men in both North and South America.

The majority of the crimes the Wild Bunch committed occurred between 1896 and 1901, and it was during this time that they moved on from horse theft, which could be cumbersome, to robbing banks and railroads. Banks were especially worth the effort to the gang because they were sure to have money and the timing was easier to predict. But it's almost certain that various members of the gang were working together in the years prior, and it's believed the Sundance Kid participated in the Great Northern Express Train Robbery in late 1892.

On November 27, 1892, Train Number 23 departed from St. Paul, headed to Butte, Montana. The train made a stop in Malta in northern Montana, as usual, but this time Sundance, William Madden, and Henry Bass got into the so-called blind baggage car. Since it was still the early morning hours before dawn in late fall Montana, the men were not seen in the darkness as the train pulled away from the station. The three outlaws pulled up their masks and directed the engineer to stop the train. Guns drawn, the engineer was told that he was not going to be harmed and that they were only there to rob the train, but the fact that their masks slipped down and gave a clear view of their faces presented a bit of a problem for them later.

The outlaws hit a small safe first, nabbing some personal effects, a check for $6.05, and $19.02 in cash. When they asked for the combination to the large safe, the engineer told them that only the agents in St. Paul at the primary stations on the route knew the combination. Unhappy with this turn of events, the outlaws told the engineer to move the train along and let him and the train go, after which the engineer was able to give a good description of the three men. When Madden and Bass were located at a saloon on December 1, they gave up Sundance as their accomplice and a wanted poster was made offering a $500 reward for the capture of Harry Longabaugh. Madden and Bass were sentenced to 10 years in prison, but they were out within three. Meanwhile, Sundance was never captured, and for the next three years he seemed to stay out of trouble. It would prove to be the calm before the storm.

Montpelier, Idaho

The first bank that Cassidy is believed to have robbed as a member of the Wild Bunch was in Montpelier, Idaho on a hot summer day. On August 13, 1896, a local storekeeper saw three men walking their horses along a street around 3:00 p.m., and he watched as they got back on their horses, rode over to the bank, and dismounted. Two men standing on the sidewalk gave them a quick glance but thought nothing of their appearance until two of the strangers pulled their bandanas over their faces and pointed revolvers at them. The robbers forced the two men inside and lined them up facing a wall with numerous customers and two of the three bank employees on duty. The assistant cashier was told to stay in place.

A man assumed to be Cassidy kept his gun pointed at the frightened people while his partner, a taller man that is believed to have been Elza Lay, relieved the bank of all its cash, gold, and silver, totaling over $7,000. When he had it all, he loaded the bags onto a pack mule and a horse. Cassidy advised the people inside to bank to wait at least 10 minutes before alerting authorities and calmly walked out the door and got on his horse. The three bandits then took off for the edge of town.

When he was sure that they were gone, the cashier ran over to the sheriff's office to tell the deputy what had happened. Though the deputy had neither a gun nor a horse and was mainly a process server, not a lawman, he was not willing to simply let the bandits get away without a chase. Thus, he hopped on a bike and headed out after the robbers. The chase was futile, but he did note that they had headed east, toward Wyoming. The only robber of the three that did not wear a mask was Bob Meeks, who did not want to attract attention while he was standing outside on the street. However, this allowed the cashier to get a good look at him, and Meeks was the only one of the three that was caught and eventually convicted of the crime.

Castle Gate, Utah

Cassidy usually did not like to rob banks or trains in Utah for fear of being recognized, but he made an exception for the Pleasant Valley Coal Company in Castle Gate and masterminded what many consider to be one of the most bold and daring crimes in American history. When it was over, he was famous on both sides of the law.

The Castle Gate mine was the largest coalmine in Carbon County, Utah. Its location in Price also made it ideal for Cassidy because it was between Robbers Roost and Brown's Hole. The large payroll that a mine of this size required made the company nervous, and the risk of outlaws lying in wait for the payroll to arrive on a scheduled train was far too great. Thus, the company had irregular paydays and tried to keep irregular schedules. Cassidy studied the train and decided that robbing the train itself was too risky, ultimately concluding that the gang would have to make their move against the paymaster.

However, without knowing exactly when the payroll would arrive, that plan required some patience. In mid-April 1897, Cassidy rode into town and asked a local barkeep if there was any work available for a rancher. He was told there might be if he waited around long enough. Cassidy thanked the man for the information and rode over to the train depot. His mare, unfamiliar with the sound of the train whistle, nearly bucked Cassidy out of his saddle. After the train departed, Cassidy went back to the saloon and worked his way through some Old Crow.

Every day for a week, Cassidy repeated the scene with every train that came into town, and his horse eventually got used to the noise from the train. On April 21, 1897 at 12:40 p.m., the train he was waiting for rolled into town. A whistle blasted to alert the miners that today would be payday, or so they thought. Cassidy saw the paymaster, E.L. Carpenter, and two assistants carry moneybags toward Carpenter's office. Carpenter was walking gingerly due to a sore toe.

Each man came out with a heavy bag. One had $700 in gold, one had $7,000 in gold, and the third had $100 in silver. As the men approached the stairs that led to their office, Carpenter felt the butt of Cassidy's revolver in his ribs. Cassidy smiled and told Carpenter that he would take the money bags and would hate to have to shoot him if he didn't comply. For a moment, Carpenter could not believe he was being robbed. Miners were everywhere, but most did not speak English and probably had no idea what was happening.

Carpenter dropped his bags and his assistant dropped the bag of silver and hid in the nearby hardware store. It occurred to Carpenter that he had seen Cassidy and one of the other men (likely Lay) earlier in the week. He noticed the horses, too, and realized that should have tipped him off. Horses were not a common sight in mining towns because the trails were too steep.

Cassidy handed Lay some of the money and got ready to mount his own horse and take off out of town, but before they did Carpenter yelled out that he had been robbed. In the chaos, Cassidy's horse got spooked and ran off, leaving Cassidy holding a bag of stolen gold with no means for a getaway. Lay was able to track the horse down, with Cassidy trailing behind on foot. Somehow, Cassidy got back on the horse, gold still in hand, and the bandits headed out of town with over $7,000. They left the bag of silver behind.

Carpenter ran for the telegraph office to alert the authorities 10 miles away in Price. However, the telegraph operator told him there was no signal because the lines had been cut. Carpenter then went to the train and told the engineer to head for Price. He didn't realize as the train steamed along the tracks that they passed Cassidy and Lay along the way.

When Carpenter got to Price, he told the sheriff what had happened, but it took several hours before the sheriff could organize a posse. Carpenter went to the telegraph office in Price to alert the other towns in the area about the presence of the bandits, but another member of the Wild Bunch, Joe Walker, had cut the telegraph wires leading out of the canyon.

A posse led by Joe Bush gave Cassidy and Lay a good chase across Utah, but Cassidy had the advantage. In addition to having planned the robbery for months, he was on his home turf. It didn't hurt that Cassidy was generous with the price he paid for fresh horses when he came across a rancher that would let him switch out his mounts. The locals felt no loyalty to the mining company and were happy to oblige the outlaws. When they had made it 70 miles across the desert to San Rafael, Cassidy and Lay met Joe Walker and split up the stolen gold coins.

Cassidy, Lay, and Walker went to Robbers Roost to hide out while the chaos died down, and the gang passed the time by gambling, drinking, racing horses, and telling stories. Ann Bassett was there with two other women, and the girls were particularly useful when the camp ran out of supplies. It was no secret to the lawmen in Utah that Cassidy and his gang were hiding out in the Robbers Roost area, but none made any attempt to ride in there. Local newspapers suggested that the sheriffs and deputies were afraid to try.

After three months of waiting, the outlaws had all they could take and decided it was time to spend some of their money. In June 1897, they went back to Brown's Hole, gathered some friends, and headed toward their favorite saloons in Wyoming. Some of the money was spent on shaves, haircuts, and new clothes. Guns were shot all in the name of fun and the bandits paid the saloonkeepers at a rate of one dollar per hole for repairs.

Belle Fourche

Belle Fourche, north of the Black Hills, saw its share of trouble in the late 19th century. In fact, the entire town nearly burned to the ground when feuding desperadoes set it ablaze in 1895. But when the Wild Bunch introduced itself to Belle Fourche on June 28, 1897, they hardly left an impression that they were a professional band of outlaws. The first error in judgment was charging Tom O'Day with the responsibility of going into town to get the lay of the land. He was a capable man when sober, but on the day before the robbery was to take place, like many other days, he had a few too many drinks. He got back to the camp too late in the day to pull off the robbery, so it had to be postponed until the next day.

When Walt Puteny, Harvey Logan, and Sundance finally made it into the Butte County Bank, one of the men drew a Colt revolver and leveled it at Art Marble, the bank's chief cashier. The bank's customers immediately put their hands into the air, as did the assistant cashier, Harry Ticknor. One of the customers, Sam Arnold, had just made his $97 deposit, and the money still sat on the counter in front of Marble, presenting an obviously tempting target. Sundance grabbed the money, but neither he nor any of the other bandits seemed to think about how it might look to someone passing by that the bank's customers were standing in plain sight with their hands thrust above their heads.

Harvey Logan, aka "Kid Curry"

As it turned out, a local merchant named Alanson Giles happened to walk by the bank and saw the robbery in progress. Giles alerted others in the area, and the street in front of the bank erupted in chaos. One member of the gang, possibly Logan, fired a shot toward the store that Giles owned, then George "Flat Nose" Curry and O'Day fired into the street. Curry stumbled around and could not get onto his horse, so he tried to steal a mule, only to discover to his horror that the mule wouldn't move. Curry was eventually caught and kept overnight in the bank vault because the nearest jail was in Deadwood, but the rest of the gang split up and Sundance made it safely back to Hole-in-the-Wall. The total haul for the botched robbery was Sam Arnold's $97, while $30,000 remained in the bank's safe.

Flat Nose Curry

Elko, Nevada

In March 1899, Sundance, Flat Nose Curry, and Kid Curry emerged from winter hiding – most likely from Hole-in-the-Wall - and reunited in Elko, Nevada. For about a week, they were seen in town along Railroad Street, the main drag, gambling and drinking and generally flaunting large amounts of cash. Perhaps they were scouting out Elko as the target of their next holdup, or maybe the idea to conduct a robbery there simply occurred to them the longer they stayed in Elko. However the plan came about, the Club Saloon's safe presented itself as a tantalizing method of financing a train robbery in Wilcox, Wyoming, something which was already in the planning stages. Sundance and his friends had heard that the safe held a large amount of cash, and they determined that robbing a saloon was going to be a lot easier than robbing a bank.

Late in the evening of Monday, April 3, the last customer out of the Club Saloon was the town constable, Joe Triplett. As Triplett made his way out, the bar's owner, E.M. James Gutridge, and the bartender, C.B. Nichols, opened up the safe behind the bar and began to count the day's receipts. At that point, Sundance, Flat Nose Curry and Kid Curry stormed into the bar with their guns drawn. Gutridge, thinking that Triplett might still be in the area, yelled for help but was bashed in the head, and one of the trio of bandits forced Gutridge and Nichols into chairs and kept a gun pointed at them while another robber kept an eye on the saloon's front door. The third outlaw scrambled behind the bar with a gunny sack and raked in all of the cash he could find, which was between $500-$3,000 according to reports. With that, they ran for the door, jumped on their horses, and headed to freedom in nearby Tuscarora.

Wilcox, Wyoming

A couple of months later, about two hours after midnight on June 2, 1899, Sundance and his cohorts set the wheels in motion for one of their most spectacular crimes. Somehow, members of the Wild Bunch received information about Union Pacific express shipments. As the first section of the Union Pacific Overland Flyer No. 1 approached the Wilcox Station in Wilcox, Wyoming, rain was pouring down from the sky and two men with red lanterns flagged down the train. The train screeched to a stop because the engineer, William R. Jones, knew that the train was approaching a wooden bridge and figured the men might be alerting him that rain had washed out the bridge.

However, after he stopped the train, the conductor saw the men draw guns, so he turned and ran back down the track to warn the second train, which would be approaching in a few minutes. The masked bandits jumped onto the train and ordered the engineer to pull it under a nearby trestle, where they had stashed a cache of dynamite, and when the conductor did not move fast enough for the robbers, one of them apparently pistol whipped the conductor. As the train cleared the bridge, one of the outlaws lit the fuse to the dynamite and set off a massive explosion. The bridge was not completely destroyed, but it was damaged enough that the second section of the train would not be able to follow them.

Jones was told to stop the first section of the train, which contained the mail and express cars, so that it could be separated from the passenger car. Jones and Dietrick did as they were told and pulled forward two miles, where four more members of the Wild Bunch were waiting. Three of them forced Jones and Dietrick to the mail car and then ordered the mail clerks to open the door. When they didn't do it, the outlaws blasted it open with dynamite. There was not much of interest in the mail car, so they moved on to the express car.

When the outlaws reached the express car, the manager of that car, Charles Woodcock, refused to open the door. Once again, the outlaws threw two sticks of dynamite at it, succeeding in blowing open the door and shaking up Woodcock enough that he couldn't remember the combination to the safe. When Woodcock didn't open the safe for them, the outlaws blew that open too, and in the process they blew off the roof and the walls of the railroad car, sending cash, bank notes and various personal items floating into the sky.

When the outlaws finally took off at 4:15 a.m., they had accumulated an array of jewelry, watches, cash, unsigned bank notes, and gold totaling approximately $50,000. The Wild Bunch was seen heading north, almost certainly toward their Hole-in-the Wall hideout, while the trainmen somehow managed to get what was left of their train to Medicine Bow about 12 miles away. At Medicine Bow, they sent a telegraph to the Union Pacific home office in Omaha, Nebraska to report the robbery and the minor wound to Jones from the blow to the head.

It was this robbery that would truly bring the Wild Bunch to the attention of the Pinkerton

Detective Agency. In the 1850s, Allan Pinkerton had established a private detective and security guard agency in Chicago, a forerunner of sorts for both private investigators and the Secret Service. A decade later, the Pinkertons, as the agency was informally called, claimed to have uncovered and thwarted a plan to assassinate President Abraham Lincoln, and from there they created the first secret service in the U.S. during the Civil War. In an effort to fight back against the notorious outlaws that targeted the nation's railroad system, railroad companies such as Union Pacific hired the Pinkertons to join forces with their own police force to capture the outlaws that preyed on their trains.

Allan Pinkerton

In the late 19th century, the Pinkertons were kept busy chasing down some of the West's most notorious outlaws. The large railroad companies, including Union Pacific, hired the Pinkertons to work with railroad detectives to protect their cargo and passengers from the robbers that were targeting their trains with alarming regularity. After a Union Pacific train was robbed in Wilcox, Wyoming, the Wild Bunch, including Butch Cassidy and the Sundance Kid, came under close surveillance of the Pinkertons. In fact, it is the detective agency that has provided some of the most detailed information about the movements of Cassidy and Sundance, although there is no source that can definitively say exactly what crimes Cassidy and Sundance actually participated in during the Wild Bunch's crime spree between 1896 and 1901.

Though there is no evidence to suggest that Butch Cassidy was part of the Wilcox robbery, it seems likely that Sundance was there. A newspaper in Rawlins, Wyoming implicated three local bandits, but the Pinkertons were not at all convinced that this was not the work of the Wild

Bunch. One of the descriptions matched that of Flat Nose, and the other two could have been Harvey Logan and his brother. Butch Cassidy had sworn to the governor of Wyoming that he would not commit any crimes there after he was given an early release from his prison sentence, and Cassidy was also not known to be violent, so the crime did not fit his modus operandi. When he saw his lawyer, William Simpson, days later and Simpson questioned him about the Wilcox robbery, Cassidy insisted he was not part of it.

That said, the Wild Bunch pooled the money from the various robberies, so it's likely Cassidy got a share of the money. It also helped the outlaws escape after their robberies. Even before conducting a robbery, Sundance and his fellow outlaws set up horse relays all along their escape route that allowed them to continue riding without having to rest their horses. They were well aware that a sheriff's posse was hot on their trail, so they stopped south of Hole-in-the-Wall near Lost Cabin to divvy up the money and go their separate ways, making it that much more difficult for the law to find them.

That posse, led by the sheriff of Converse County, Josiah Hazen, finally caught up with three of them on June 6 at Castle Creek, which was renamed Teapot Dome several years later. The area is a deep ravine with plenty of rocks for hiding, making Hazen a sitting duck when he rode right up toward Kid Curry, who shot and killed him in a gun battle. The rest of the posse hid while the outlaws got away.

Sundance was never arrested for the crime and neither were any of his accomplices, leading to plenty of speculation that they received a great deal of help from local ranchers in Wyoming who had little love for local law enforcement. Small ranchers were in a battle with the larger ranching outfits that were springing up in the Wyoming prairie, and the law was seen as a friend to the wealthier ranching companies. J. Elmer Brock, a local rancher near Powder River, said in a book he wrote on the local history that Sundance was among the men that rode through his family's ranch after getting fresh horses at the nearby Billy Hill Ranch. Brock said that a posse also spent a night at his family's ranch, and the next day all of their food and blankets were gone. Brock wrote, "Isn't it strange that as many outlaws as had been in that place that the first people to commit petty larceny should be a bunch of United States Marshals?"[3] Such was the attitude of many of the locals.

Cassidy's Attempt at Amnesty

In many ways, Cassidy proved himself to be cut from a different mold than other outlaws. He was a congenial man who had many friends who were not outlaws. During times when he was on the run, he was able to mix and mingle with relative ease among the law-abiding locals. Wherever he went, whether it was his ranch in Dubois or his ranch in Argentina, he got along with his neighbors and was respected as a hard-working man. If he did not want to live the

---

[3] Donna Ernst, *Wild West Magazine.*

fugitive's life, it would come as no surprise.

In 1899, Cassidy visited the office of attorney Orlando Powers in Ogden, Utah. The two men did not know each other, but they knew of each other from when Cassidy financed the defense of Matt Warner, E.B. Coleman, and Dave Wall. The men had been charged with murder in a mining claim dispute in Vernal, Utah, and the money used for their defense most likely came from the bank robbery in Montpelier.

Cassidy laid out his case for Powers. He explained that he was being portrayed as a vicious outlaw and had been given a reputation that was different from reality. He told Powers that he had never committed murder and only robbed banks and trains, not people. He appealed to Powers, who he buttered up by calling him the best lawyer in Utah, to make an arrangement with the governor to grant Cassidy amnesty or perhaps allow him to plead guilty to lesser charges. If he could get a deal like that, Cassidy said, he would go straight and leave his life of crime behind.

Powers reportedly said that it was unlikely that such a deal could be granted. Cassidy was wanted for too many crimes by large companies, and even if Cassidy claimed that there were no witnesses who could be used against him in court, those companies would have found someone. He advised Cassidy that his best bet was to go back in hiding.

Cassidy did not stop with Powers, however. His next visit was to Parley P. Christensen, an attorney in Salt Lake City. Christensen, a graduate of Cornell University School of Law and one of the brightest young politicians in the Republican Party, knew Governor Heber Wells. They were both delegates at the state constitutional convention in 1895 and Christensen later served on the Utah legislature. Cassidy hoped that Christensen's personal connection with Wells would boost his chances at getting a deal.

Christensen

After meeting with Christensen, Cassidy had some hope. Wells agreed to a meeting with Cassidy, and after hearing his proposal Wells said that if there were no murder warrants against him, they could work out a deal. Cassidy, sure that there would be no such warrants, was confident that a deal would be made, but when Utah's district attorney checked Cassidy's record, he did find his name on a murder warrant. At Cassidy's second meeting with the governor, he told him about the warrant and said that he would not be able to make a deal. Cassidy was incredulous and insisted that he never killed a man, but Wells explained that all that was needed was for his name to appear on a warrant. With all of the bank and train robberies that were occurring, the Wild Bunch was usually considered the top band of suspects. On top of that, it would have been easy for Cassidy's name to surface anytime other members of the Wild Bunch pulled a job and killed someone in the aftermath. If someone said they say Butch Cassidy was on the scene or suspected him of being there, his name could easily be on a warrant.

Governor Wells

It was at this point that Powers had another idea for Cassidy. He proposed the idea of Cassidy not only agreeing to stop living a life of crime but work as an express guard for the Union Pacific Railroad. If he agreed to this, perhaps Union Pacific would agree to drop their charges against him. Powers felt that this would allow the railroad to keep close tabs on Cassidy, as well as possibly serve as a deterrent against further attacks if other bandits knew he was on the train.

Despite the fact that such an arrangement would do nothing to eliminate the charges against Cassidy from other railroad lines or from the growing list of states in which he was wanted, there is evidence to suggest that Cassidy may have accepted the deal. A letter dated May 30, 1900 addressed to Governor Wells was located in the governor's collection of papers in the Utah State Archives. The letter was from W.S. Seavey, an agent for the Thiel Detective Service's Denver office and the former chief of police for the Omaha Police Department. Seavey said, "I desire to inform you that I have reliable information to the effect that if the authorities will let him alone and the UPRR officials will give him a job as guard, etc., the outlaw Butch Cassidy will lay down his arms, come in, give himself up, go to work and be a good peacable [sic] citizen hereafter."[4]

For reasons that are not clear, the deal never happened. For many years, rumors persisted that the Union Pacific officials stood Cassidy up, prompting him to write a note telling the railroad executives what they could do with their deal. However, historians have determined that no such note likely ever existed. It is more likely that if such as deal was under consideration, the railroad understood that it presented too much risk and not enough reward for them. They had long viewed Harvey Logan (Kid Curry) as far more dangerous than Butch Cassidy, and they might rightly have wondered how Cassidy would have been able to hold Logan or any other member of the Wild Bunch off if they tried to rob one of their trains. There would also have obviously been questions about whether or not Cassidy could be trusted to not divulge the details of payroll trains to his associates. Certainly the railroad's board of directors, who had paid $110 million to buy the company in 1893, would have had reservations about letting one of the West's most notorious outlaws guard their investment.

Chapter 7: Heading to South America

Legend has attached the names of Butch Cassidy and the Sundance Kid to a variety of crimes after the Wilcox robbery. The most famous crimes were the Tipton, Wyoming train robbery in August 1900 and the Winnemucca Bank holdup in September 1900, but there is no evidence that they were there. Cassidy had experienced too many close calls, and after a failed attempt at getting amnesty from the state of Utah, he knew that he was running out of luck.

At some point during that year, Cassidy proposed the idea of heading south of the border to South America, and Argentina was especially appealing for an outlaw looking for a new start. The economy was strong, and the ranching life was not too far removed from what a cowboy was used to. Everything was new, much like in the western U.S., and it had every sign of being a prosperous country on the strength of its agriculture industry.

Cassidy suggested going to Argentina to some of his Wild Bunch friends, but the only two who were interested in the plan were Kid Curry and Sundance. Kid Curry ultimately passed, but Sundance was in. On November 21, 1900, some members of the gang, including Sundance, Cassidy, and Kid Curry, had a last hurrah in Texas. They visited the red light districts to enjoy the liquor, the gambling, and the women. They also stopped in at John Swartz's photography studio and, dressed in their finest suits, had their photo taken. Swartz displayed the photo, which has been widely reproduced in the century since it was taken, on the window of his studio, having no idea that the five men he had photographed were wanted criminals. The photo found its way to the Pinkertons, who were grateful for the headshots to include on their wanted posters.

---

[4] Patterson, Richard. "Butch Cassidy's Surrender Offer." *True West Magazine,* June 12, 2006.

Sitting (L-R): Sundance Kid, Ben Kilpatrick (The Tall Texan), and Butch Cassidy
Standing (L-R): Will Carver (News Carver), and Harvey Logan (Kid Curry)

With operatives spread across North America and eventually South America, the Pinkertons had the ability to track the Wild Bunch when the trail went cold for law enforcement. Charlie Siringo, working under the alias Charles L. Carter on behalf of the Pinkertons, managed to infiltrate the Wild Bunch after the Wilcox robbery, and information obtained by Siringo put the heat on several members of the Wild Bunch. This resulted in the capture of Kid Curry, who was killed in a shootout in Colorado in 1904. Though not the most notorious of the gang, Kid Curry was the most feared, and it is believed he killed nearly 10 law enforcement officers in his short life. After he was captured in Tennessee, he headed to Montana and murdered a rancher who he claimed killed his brother years earlier. He was captured in Tennessee and escaped a second time, only to finally be killed in the Colorado shootout.

Cassidy and Sundance had split up after their excursion to Texas and planned to reconnect in New York on February 1, 1902, but Sundance did not arrive in the Big Apple alone. Sundance came east with the most mysterious of all the members of the Wild Bunch, a young woman best known today as Etta Place. The name and fate of Etta Place has remained one of the most enduring mysteries of the Butch and Sundance legend, and aside from the fact she was a long-time companion of Sundance's, little else is known about her. Whoever she was, Etta Place was using the maiden name of Sundance's mother (Annie Place), and she was referred to at times as Mrs. Harry Longabaugh or Mrs. Harry A. Place. She also once signed her name "Mrs. Ethel Place".

In fact, Etta Place is such a mystery that not even the Pinkertons knew if that was her real name. Since some have speculated that Etta was a music teacher, the connection is made back to Ethel Bishop, a music teacher in San Antonio. There are some who believe that Etta, who the Pinkertons called Ethel, was actually Ann Basset, but this was never confirmed. Although the pictures of Etta and Ann look strikingly alike, authorities strongly believe that Etta Place was with Sundance in South America from 1902-1904, while Ann was arrested for rustling cattle in Utah in 1903. Assuming she wasn't Ann Bassett, Etta Place was only one of five known women allowed in Robbers Roost, including the Bassett sisters, Elzy Lay's girlfriend Maude Davis, and gang member Laura Bullion.

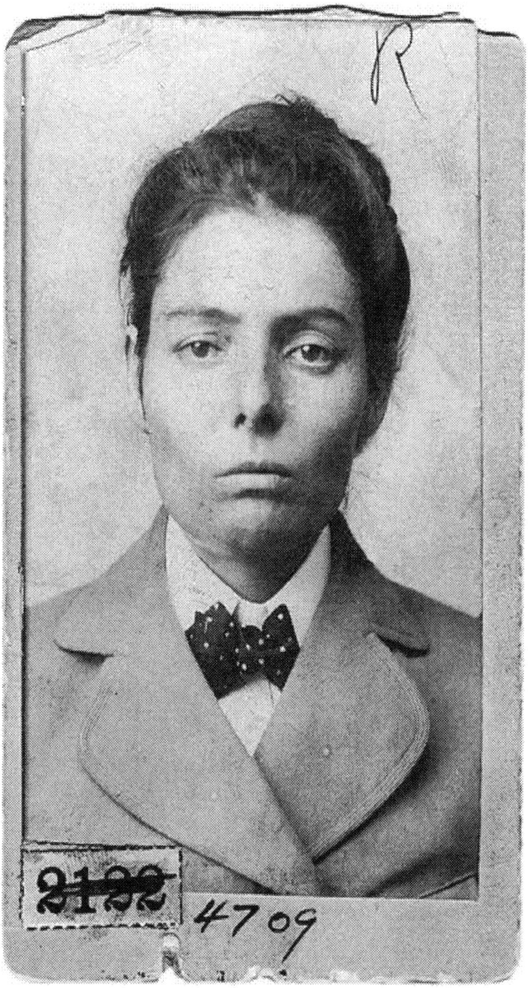

The Pinkerton Agency's mugshot of Laura Bullion

There was speculation that Etta Place may have been Eunice Gray, who operated a house of ill repute in Fort Worth, but Gray never claimed to be Etta Place. A reporter simply speculated that after she said she had been in the Fort Worth area since 1901, aside from a brief trip to South America for a couple of years.

According to Donna Ernst, the Sundance Kid's biographer and niece, she looked at the records for every woman named Ethel born between 1875 and 1880 in San Antonio and Fort Worth, This was because, in addition to Etta, the Pinkertons referred to her as Ethel, Rita, and Eva Place. Ernst eliminated every woman named Ethel she uncovered in that timeframe other than Ethel

Bishop, but this is still a stretch because there is no solid reason to believe that Etta Place's real first name is Etta. As for her place of birth, the Pinkertons believed it was Texas, as they had a lead suggesting that her parents were from there, but those that met Etta believed that she was from the East Coast.

Certainly, Etta exuded a certain sense of refinement in her speech and appearance. While in New York City, Sundance and Etta went to the DeYoung Photography Studio and had their portrait taken. Both looked like two of the city's most proper citizens, right down to the Tiffany watch that is pinned to Etta's dress. Neighbors that knew Etta and Sundance in South America recalled seeing Etta ride her horse English style, but despite her apparent cultured style, there were rumors that she was at one point in the employ of Ms. Fannie Porter of San Antonio, who ran one of the most upscale bordellos in all of the West. The Pinkertons interviewed her about what she might know about Etta Place, but she claimed ignorance. However, another of Porter's ladies did talk to the Pinkertons, and whatever she said led them to believe that Etta Place was once a prostitute there.

Sundance Kid and Etta Place before they headed to South America

What is known is that upon their arrival in New York City, Sundance and Etta presented themselves as Mr. and Mrs. Harry Place. Those that accept Etta Place as her real name conclude that she was Sundance's cousin, and it's been suggested that she was calling herself Etta Place because she and Sundance were married. Perhaps it signified nothing other than an alias for both of them. The Pinkertons said that the one photo that exists of the two was their wedding photo, but there are no records indicating that the two were married.

Before they made it to New York, Etta and Sundance rang in the New Year at New Orleans and then took a train to Pennsylvania to see Sundance's family in early 1901. Sundance introduced Etta to his sister and brothers as his wife and reportedly also told them that he wanted to go straight, which was the reason he was going to South America. He incorrectly presumed he would be away from the watchful eyes of the Pinkertons outside of the country.

The fact that Etta was with Butch Cassidy and Sundance strengthens the argument that they were not planning any more escapades in South America. Cassidy did not like having women around when they were planning a job, presumably because of the distraction they presented to the men.

Mr. and Mrs. Harry Place, along with "Jim Ryan," Cassidy's alias, checked into a boarding house in New York. They played the roles of a Wyoming cattle buyer, his wife, and his brother-in-law, who were there to do sightseeing in the big city. They rented the second-floor suite and stayed there for nearly three weeks. On February 20, 1901, the trio boarded the ship *Herminus,* bound for Argentina.

One of the first things that Cassidy and Sundance did when they arrived in Buenos Aires was to visit the London and Platte River Bank, where Sundance made a $12,000 deposit so that they could put in a land claim. When their application was approved, they settled in Cholilo in May. They bought sixteen horses on June 11, and in October they went to the capital of Rawson to register their brands. In March 1902, Cassidy and Sundance applied to homestead four leagues of land, or approximately 17,000 acres.

For the most part, Butch, Sundance and Etta did nothing to indicate that they would cause their neighbors any difficulties. However, a photo historian named Ricardo Vallmitjana noted that they actually brought a great deal of fear to the area at first because they wore their guns everywhere, and the locals came to fear all North Americans because of Cassidy and Sundance. Residents of the region relaxed for a while, but then Cassidy and Sundance were blamed for a local murder – one they could not have committed because they were in all likelihood dead – and it caused more distrust of North Americans.

If Cassidy and Sundance thought moving south of the border was going to shake the Pinkertons from their tails, they were mistaken. The Pinkertons knew that they were with Etta Place in Buenos Aires, and in July 1903 the chief of the Buenos Aires police force received a letter from Robert Pinkerton. He advised him that the bandits were in their vicinity and included the most recent photographs that the agency had on file, as well as descriptions. The Pinkertons had operatives in South America and asked an agent in Argentina to go to their ranch and arrest them, but the operative said it would have to wait. It was the rainy season and he could not easily travel inland, but the police chief did agree to monitor the three in case they tried to leave Argentina.

Much to the frustration of the Pinkertons, they would later come to find out that Etta and Sundance were right under their nose at one point. The two of them had returned to New York

City on the *Soldier Prince* and arrived on April 3, 1902, signing in at a boarding house on the Lower East Side as Mr. and Mrs. Harry Place. Among their excursions was a trip to Coney Island, a trip to Atlantic City to meet up with Sundance's brother Harvey, and a trip to Pennsylvania, presumably to visit his sister. They may have also made their way to Chicago for Sundance to get treated for an old gunshot wound to his leg. Before leaving on the return trip to Argentina, they made another stop at Tiffany's and purchased a watch for $15.35. They did not leave until July, meaning that they had been in the U.S. for three months without being detected by the Pinkertons.

Chapter 8: The End of the Road?

The outlaws would spend more than 7 years in South America, the first five of which they spent without apparently committing any crimes. For that reason, it is unclear what sent Cassidy and Sundance back to a life of crime in 1906. For the most part, they had blended in easily with Cholilo after the locals got used to them, and they were known as Santiago Ryan and Enrique Place. The territorial governor, Julio Lezana, even spent a night in their log cabin home in 1904, and Etta reportedly danced with him as Sundance played the guitar.

Whatever the circumstances, Cassidy, Sundance, and Etta lived a life of relative peace until the spring of 1906. It is not clear if they heard that the Pinkertons were going to make a move or if they simply got the urge to resume their criminal ways, but with Etta calmly holding the horses, an American fugitive helped Cassidy and Sundance rob a bank in Mercedes of $20,000. One of the three men killed the banker in the process before they split the proceeds and went their separate ways.

When the local newspaper ran a story about the robbery along with photos of Butch and Sundance, including a mention that the robbers spoke English, they were also suspected of a robbery in Rio Gallegos. That robbery set off reports that they were also involved in other robberies throughout South America, including banks at Bahia Blanca and a payroll train at Eucalyptus. They were even accused of killing a man in Arroyo Pescado in 1910, but this seems unlikely because murder was not their style, and, more importantly, it is highly likely that they were dead by then. Regardless of their actual involvement, the aftermath of the bank robbery at Mercedes meant Cassidy and Sundance were on the run again.

In the meantime, what became of Etta Place is a mystery. The last written record of her is at Arroyo Pescado, and then she disappeared from the records, despite the fact that the Pinkerton agency was supposedly keeping close tabs on her. Some historians believe she died in South America too, but a woman matching her physical description tried to get documentation legally declaring Harry Longabaugh dead in 1909. After that request was denied, that was the last the public saw or heard from Etta Place.

Of course, there were also many in law enforcement that had given up on the idea of catching Cassidy and Sundance as well, since they always seemed to be a step ahead of the people that were chasing them. However, their luck would seemingly run out in late 1908. Earlier in that year, the payroll for the Aramayo mines, located in the southern region of Bolivia, was robbed. That is a fact, but what happened after that is up for debate. Most historians agree that Cassidy and Sundance made their way to San Vicente on November 6. The local justice, known as the corregidor, made arrangements for them to stay in a spare room at the home of a local villager. Some say that it was a mule that gave them away to the corregidor. Cassidy and Sundance had taken the equipment off of their horses and mules, setting it all aside and letting the animals graze. Supposedly, the corregidor watched one of the mules roll on its back in the dust and recognized it as an animal that belonged to his friend. The mule had been used to transport the payroll to the Aramayo mines. He was suspicious, but also found the casual manner of Cassidy and Sundance to be unusual if they were, indeed, responsible for the robbery.

He alerted four members of the Bolivian cavalry, including a captain, that the Aramayo mine bandits may be in town. Soon after that, one of the soldiers entered a room where Cassidy and Sundance were staying – some say that they were fueling up on food and whiskey – but he was met by Cassidy, who shot and killed him. If true, this is believed to be the only man Cassidy ever killed. The other two men took cover and fired into the room. In the mean time, the captain instructed the corregidor to round up men from the village to surround the building to keep Cassidy and Sundance from escaping.

There are different versions of what may have happened next. There are reports that Sundance ran out onto the patio, shooting as he went, hoping to reach the rifles that were leaning along a wall. He was shot before he reached the end of the courtyard. Cassidy ran out to get him, taking more than one bullet himself, and dragged the mortally wounded Sundance back inside. There are also reports that shortly after the captain arrived, three loud screams were heard coming from the building, followed by silence.

The Bolivian army reported that when they finally entered the room they found the men believed to be Butch and Sundance dead. Sundance's body had several gunshot wounds to the arms and one to the forehead, while Cassidy had a wound to an arm and had also been shot in the temple. The Bolivians concluded that Cassidy put Sundance out of his misery before turning the gun on himself because they were out of ammunition. However, there are also reports that they had plenty of ammunition and Sundance even had a rifle nearby. The outlaws did have the money from the Aramayo mine, as well as map of Bolivia, and the payroll officer confirmed that the dead men were the same men that committed the robbery. An inquest was held, but Bolivian officials never officially identified the names of the dead bandits, who were quickly buried in the San Vicente cemetery.

Reports soon got back to friends of Cassidy and Sundance in Bolivia that they had died in San Vicente, and the last reported sighting of them was at the Hotel Terminus in Tupiza. A friend greeted Cassidy as Mr. Maxwell, one of his aliases, but Cassidy reportedly said that he was now going by Santiago Lowe. A man by that name was, indeed, a guest of the hotel that night. None of the newspaper articles about the incident ever referred to the outlaws by name, nor did they speculate that the famous Butch Cassidy and Sundance Kid had met their demise in the gun battle.

It was not until a wire service story out of Argentina suggested that the two unnamed bandits were the same men who robbed a bank in Mercedes that the Cassidy/Sundance connection was made. The first English account of the shootout in San Vicente came in "Across South America," a 1911 travelogue by Hiram Bingham. In 1913, A.G. Francis wrote "The End of an Outlaw" for *World Wide Magazine* and discussed his encounters with Cassidy and who he identified as Kid Curry, rather than Sundance. Some of the information was accurate, but the Pinkerton agency declared that the article was fiction. Books followed in 1922 and 1924 that discussed the shootout in San Vicente, but details were still vague. In 1930, a friend of Cassidy, Percy Seiber, granted an interview to Arthur Chapman for an article for *The Elks Magazine.* Seiber gave Chapman a glorified account of the shootout, and it is believed he was the first one to suggest that Cassidy and Sundance faced an army of Bolivian soldiers rather than four men and some villagers as backup. He also put Cassidy and Sundance at crimes that they could not possibly have committed. Still, historians referred to the article as fact for years, and when William Goldman wrote the screenplay for the 1969 movie *Butch Cassidy and the Sundance Kid*, he used two books that incorporated the fabrications from Seiber as reference material.

Despite the lack of confirmation, in July 1909 Frank Aller, Sundance's benefactor, wrote to Bolivian authorities requesting death certificates for Americans, one called Frank Boyd or H.A. Brown, the other by the name of Maxwell. One of Cassidy's known aliases was Maxwell. The Americans were supposedly killed in San Vicente and buried as unknowns. Boyd – presumably Sundance – had an estate in Chile that needed to be settled. The birth certificates that were finally sent to Aller from the Bolivian foreign minister in 1910 listed the names of the dead as "unknown" and included a copy of the police investigation from the San Vicente shootout.

Many believe that Butch Cassidy and the Sundance Kid did not die in Bolivia but actually returned to the United States and lived to ripe old ages. There were alleged sightings across the world, including Mexico, France, Ireland, Idaho, Georgia, and Washington. No American newspapers ever published obituaries or gave any type of account of the Bolivian gun battle, although the Bolivian papers had several stories about the shootout. News about two of the most notorious outlaws of the era simply stopped. Rumors of Sundance's death simply spread among his circle of friends in 1909 when mail sent to him in Chile went unanswered.

The most enduring rumor about Sundance's return to the United States is that he lived out his life as William Henry Long in Utah. Long committed suicide near Duchesne, Utah on November 27, 1936. Etta Forsyth, who was 91 years old in 2008, said that her "Uncle Billy" married her grandmother, a widow with six children. Forsyth's daughter, Dianne, told a local newspaper that her grandmother believed that Long was an old Wild West outlaw but did not know for sure which outlaw he claimed to be. In December 2008, with a documentary crew filming, Long's body was exhumed so that his remains could be tested and potentially matched with DNA from the Forsyth family. The Forsyths are Mormons, and it was an important aspect of their faith to complete their genealogy records on Long, whose true background had stumped them.

John M. McCullough, a biological anthropologist from Utah State University, said that he examined a photograph of Sundance and compared it to a photograph of Long. He said in court, "It is clear that these two photographs are of the (same) person,"[5] giving the court reason to grant the request to exhume Long's skeletal remains. It was not the first time that Long's remains had been examined. Family members had DNA testing done on his skull and femur years earlier, but the test results were not known. The results of the 2008 test were determined to be inconclusive.

Jerry Nickle, who has published a website insisting that Long and Harry Longabaugh are one and the same, said that he was disappointed in the results because he is certain that Long is Sundance. He recalls that as a child, he heard several stories about Long robbing trains and banks with Butch Cassidy. Nickle also claims that the Pinkerton notes confirm his belief. Facts such as both men having sinus difficulties and similar leg wounds due to gunshots, as well as their year of birth, strengthen his beliefs.

Dan Buck and Anne Meadows are not inclined to agree with Nickle. The authors of *Digging Up Butch and Sundance* have uncovered 60 different versions of how Butch and Sundance met their demise. Buck said he has not seen anything in the Pinkerton files that indicates that Long is Sundance, calling Long a "pretender." Buck and Meadows have spent a great deal of time in South America investigating the movements of the two outlaws during that period of their lives. Not surprisingly, Buck insists the fact that nobody knows exactly where they were buried has fueled many of the rumors that the outlaws survived the gun battle.

Chapter 9: The Legacy of Butch and Sundance

America's fascination with the Wild West era has continued on into the 21st century, and the fact that Butch Cassidy and the Sundance Kid are two of the most popular icons of that legendary period in American history can largely be attributed to the power of pop culture. Even though Cassidy and Sundance were not together often during the Wild Bunch crime sprees, and despite the fact that they had committed a grand total of two robberies in the eight years that they lived in South America, they have since been portrayed as inseparable bandits responsible for an array of heists, holdups, and robberies.

---

[5] Geoff Liesek, "Is Sundance Really Buried in Duchesne?"

In the century since their alleged shootout in Bolivia, the silver screen has ensured that one can hardly be discussed without the other. The first sighting of the two men in film was in 1951 in *Texas Rangers*. Ian McDonald, a steely-eyed actor who appeared in several westerns, played Sundance to John Doucette's Butch Cassidy. In 1956, Alan Hale, Jr., best known as the Skipper on the sitcom *Gilligan's Island*, took his turn at playing Sundance in *The Three Outlaws*. In the 2011 film *Blackthorn*, screenwriter Miguel Barros wrote a story that the outlaws survived the shootout in Bolivia.

The most popular portrayal of the two, and the film that can largely be credited for making Butch Cassidy and the Sundance Kid household names was the 1969 film *Butch Cassidy and the Sundance Kid*. Goldman, who sold his screenplay for $400,000 in a bidding war won by 20th Century Fox, crafted two characters that appear playful and dangerous. The quick banter between the two also suggests that Cassidy and Sundance were close friends whose rightful ending would be to die together. The reality is that Cassidy was much closer friends with fellow outlaw Elzy Lay.

The film gave moviegoers an entirely new type of Western. It was smart and sophisticated, but it could hardly be described as dark. The fact that one of the most popular and handsome actors of the 20th century, Paul Newman, was cast as Cassidy did not hurt the movie's box office receipts, either. Newman wanted Jack Lemmon to play Sundance, which gives some insight into the humor that was injected into the dialogue, but ultimately Sundance was played by an unknown actor named Robert Redford. The movie went on to be considered a classic, winning Goldman an Academy Award for Best Screenplay in 1970. It was also was chosen by the Library of Congress for preservation by the National Film Registry in 2003. Few could have predicted the acclaim, considering the fact that many movie executives expected it to be a flop and were not sure that audiences would believe the story even if it was based in fact.

With interest in Cassidy and Sundance revived, a slew of books and magazine articles followed the movie, although most were sloppy and had little credible research to back up their claims that the outlaws lived out their final years in the U.S. One person who fueled the fire on the idea that Cassidy at least returned to the U.S. is his sister, Lula Parker Betenson. Butch left the family home in Utah when Lula was a baby, but she wrote a book in 1975 that chronicled the life of her family and her famous brother's exploits, including the claim that he returned to visit the family in 1925. Lula never did reveal the alias that her brother was using, but she did say that he lived in Spokane, Washington, although he was not the same man in Spokane who got his 15 minutes of fame by stating he was the "real" Butch Cassidy.

Understandably, her claim caught the attention of historians, who visited with Lula to get more information but came away with the impression that Lula knew very little about Cassidy. One of her sons simply said that she made up the fact that he had visited in 1925. Later, Lula said that she was just having some fun with the stories. What is probably most important is that if Cassidy was still alive, he never visited his father, who lived to be 94 years old and spent a considerable amount of time searching for his son when it was not clear what had happened to him. Those who suggest Cassidy wouldn't have visited his father point out that he was aware that the Pinkerton agency would have likely found out if he reached out to his father.

Butch and Sundance have also earned immortality in museums. Crook County seems to have forgiven Sundance for his crimes in Wyoming, and a statute of the legendary outlaw striking a relaxed pose on a bench is on the courthouse lawn and has become a popular photo spot for tourists. Inside the Crook County Museum is an exhibit about the most famous trial in the county's history. In Fort Worth, visitors can stay at Etta's Place, a bed and breakfast located in Sundance Square, which is in a neighborhood that was called Hell's Half Acre in Sundance's heyday. Each of the 10 rooms is named for a member of the Wild Bunch.

San Vicente, today still a town of just 800 people, has also attempted to cash in on its place in the history of the Wild West history. The Butch Cassidy and Sundance Kid Memorial opened in the fall of 2009 in the poorest area of the country, and the road to the museum is not even paved. To visit the museum, one must first locate the woman who has the keys, and she will also serve as the tour guide. There is not much more to it than some photos and a few antique guns, but it is hoped that the museum will bring some income to the region.

The fascination with Butch Cassidy and the Sundance Kid in popular culture is not difficult to understand. They were two of the last of the notorious Western outlaws to die with their "boots on", and they lived and died in a time of rapid change in American society. Even the 1969 movie pays homage to this with a scene in which Cassidy and Sundance express dismay at the cold, impersonal nature of banks. Of course, these banks were also catching up to the likes of the Wild Bunch with technology, making the life of bank robbers that much more challenging.

Together, the two outlaws remain a major part of American pop culture, with their images largely comprised of myth and mystery. The mystery surrounding their deaths is part of the allure. Did Sundance want to leave behind a life of crime and go straight when he made it to South America with Etta and Butch? It is certainly possible. Not only were his chances of beating the odds and staying either alive or out of jail getting slimmer, times were changing. The U.S. was in the midst of leaving its Wild West roots behind and forging ahead into an industrial era. There were fewer places for an old horseman and outlaw to make a living.

Nobody knows for sure why Butch Cassidy and the Sundance Kid went back to being criminals, but what is certain is that there are many people who hope they did not die in Bolivia and that instead, two of America's favorite bandits got a chance to live their final years in peace. Despite the fact that Butch and Sundance were criminals, the glimpses of their character that come through in stories about their lives demonstrate that they had the kind of swagger, charm, courage, and ability (or luck) to escape the law that Americans have come to associate with so many legends of the West. The same traits that made them two of the West's most successful outlaws will also ensure that Butch and Sundance continue to be two of the most romanticized figures of that era.

Bibliography

Drago, Gail. *Etta Place: Her Life and Times with Butch Cassidy and the Sundance Kid.* Plano, TX: Republic of Texas Press. 1996.

Ernst, Donna B. "The Wilcox Train Robbery." *Wild West Magazine.* June 12, 2006. http://www.historynet.com/the-wilcox-train-robbery.htm

Ernst, Donna B. *The Sundance Kid: The Life of Harry Alonzo Longabaugh.* Norman, OK: University of Oklahoma Press. 2009.

Kelly, Charles. The Outlaw Trail: A History of Butch Cassidy and his Wild Bunch. Lincoln, NE: University of Nebraska Press. 1996 (reprinted edition).

Liesek, Geoff. "Is Sundance Really Buried in Duchesne?" *Deseret News.* December 16, 2008.

Liesek, Geoff. "Legend of Sundance Lives On." *Deseret News.* January 3, 2010. http://trib.com/news/state-and-regional/article_39420cdc-e867-50e6-a33c-25bd0ecb41cb.html.

Patterson, Richard. "Butch Cassidy's Surrender Offer." *True West Magazine.* June 12, 2006.

Patterson, Richard. Butch Cassidy: A Biography. Lincoln, NE: University of Nebraska Press. 1998.

Rutter, Michael. Outlaw Tails of Utah: True Stories of Utah's Most Famous Rustlers, Robbers, and Bandits. Guilford, CT: Globe Pequot Press.

Slatta, Richard W. *The Mythical West: An Encyclopedia of Legend, Lore, and Popular Culture.* Santa Barbara: ABC-CLIO. 2001.

Printed in Great Britain
by Amazon

58401163R00025